QUAINT FURNITURE

IN

ARTS AND CRAFTS

Genuine Russia and Spanish
Morocco Leather

RUSSIAN HAND BEATEN COPPER

ELECTRIC FIXTURES, LIBRARY SETS,
SMOKING SETS, AND A LARGE LINE
OF ODD PIECES BOTH USEFUL AND
ORNAMENTAL.

IN PRESENTING this catalogue of Quaint Furniture in Arts and Crafts—illustrating the most complete and representative line of its class manufactured by any one house—brief reference may properly be made to the fundamental principles underlying this new period of furniture and decoration.

SIMPLICITY   DURABILITY

HARMONY   COMFORT

INEXPENSIVENESS

Quaint Furniture in Arts and Crafts has conclusively disproven the mistaken impression that ornament is beauty. Its plain surfaces, simple, graceful outlines, and rich, soft colors are beautiful enough without ornament. And to the harmony of form and color is added a harmony of style and atmosphere to a degree impossible with any other period, classic or modern, under existing decorative conditions.

Passing from the artistic to the material, this same twentieth century Quaint Furniture in Arts and Crafts is the veritable embodiment of comfort. It is a tribute to the materialistic spirit of the age that the artist and artisan, when they joined hands in the evolution of this style, did not withhold consideration of bodily ease—indeed, disproved the sometime theory that ugliness must be synonymous with comfort.

There is no type or kind of furniture as well constructed as Quaint Furniture in Arts and Crafts. Only the best material is used, and the most skilled workmen are employed exclusively. Quality is always sought, even in the most trivial details. All drawer ends are solid black walnut. The joints are all the old fashioned tongue-and-groove kind, first made by the methodical German artisan, and really not equaled by any modern device. We have never known of an open joint with this construction, so we easily guarantee our manufacture. The leather used is the famous Russian and Spanish morocco, made only from goat and calf skin, and is guaranteed for five years.

There is no reason why artistic merit should necessarily imply great cost. Yet many people have assumed that an artistic home must in the very nature of things mean an expensive one. They forget that a medium priced article may possess artistic merit, as well as one of high price—that there are now as beautiful colors in cotton as in silk, and as graceful shapes in oak as in mahogany. Given the true artist's sense of proportion and a discriminating eye for effect, the designer will make a thing of beauty out of a common stool; without these qualities he will make something ugly and common that may cost even more than the other. Quaint Furniture in Arts and Crafts has made ideals possible which might otherwise have been impossible—has brought within the means of those with even the most moderate of incomes the possibility of artistic homes. The decorative feature is simplified—no longer requires the presence of an unlimited purse to make the fulfillment of the artistic home possible. The style lends itself happily to the most inexpensive of furnishings, requiring only the keynote of harmony and simplicity, shows no effort toward the artistic, but simply is artistic. With the added touch of individuality, the simplest home may be made far more truly artistic than the furnished house of which the cost was unlimited.

Quaint Furniture in Arts and Crafts is made for every room in the home, as well as for the club, the cafe, the hotel. The characteristics of rooms furnished throughout with this furniture are restfulness, beauty and harmony.

RUSSIAN HAND-BEATEN COPPER

All of these goods—which are so especially well adapted to accompany the Quaint Furniture in Arts and Crafts—are strictly hand made, no machinery of any kind whatever being used in their manufacture. The workmanship is of the best which can be produced by the skilled copper beaters employed in these shops. We know there is much in heredity, and these workmen have not only been employed many years at the same trade, but this experience is augmented by the teachings of their fathers, and their fathers' fathers—all copper workers for generations—rendering these craftsmen unequaled in their line, and the individuality of whose work is manifest in each and every piece that comes from their hands.

MEASUREMENTS

In giving dimensions, we have stated the outside measurements for settees; inside measurements for all chairs and rockers. All other measurements given are self-explanatory.

No goods sold at retail—all orders must come through furniture dealers.

NO. 3911 SETTEE.

Height, 36 in.; Depth, 30 in.; Length, 84 in.
Hand Laced Loose Seat and Back Cushions.   Oak, $125.00

All Oak furniture finished in Fumed Oak or any other finish desired.

Spanish Morocco Leather made from Goat and Calfskin is the only leather used on these goods. All leather guaranteed for five years. No roan or sheepskin used because of poor wearing qualities.

3911

NO. 780½ MORRIS CHAIR.

Height, 36 in.; Width, 20 in.; Depth, 21 in.
Loose Seat and Back Cushions.   Oak, $31.00

NO. 385 MORRIS CHAIR.

Height, 38 in.; Width, 21 in.; Depth, 22 in.
Loose Seat and Back Cushions.   Oak, $40.00

NO. 631 MORRIS ROCKER.

Height, 36 in.; Width, 21 in.; Depth, 21 in.
Hand Laced Loose Seat and Back Cushions.   Oak, $54.00
No. 631½ Morris Chair to match above,   52.00

NO. 323 ROCKER.

Height, 40 in.; Width, 22 in.; Depth, 23 in.
Hand Laced Loose Seat and Back Cushions.   Oak, $60.00
No. 323½ Arm Chair to match above,   60.00

NO. 343 MORRIS CHAIR.

Height, 38 in.; Width, 21 in.; Depth, 22 in.
Hand Laced Loose Seat and Back Cushions.   Oak, $52.00

All Oak furniture finished in Fumed Oak or any other
finish desired.

Spanish Morocco Leather made from Goat and Calfskin
is the only leather used on these goods. All leather guaranteed for five years. No roan or sheepskin used because
of poor wearing qualities.

8

343

385

780½

631

323

9

NO. 3715 SETTEE.

Height, 34 in.; Depth, 30 in.; Length, 72 in.
Hand Laced Loose Seat and Back Cushions.   Oak, $114.00

All Oak furniture finished in Fumed Oak or any other finish desired.

Spanish Morocco Leather made from Goat and Calfskin is the only leather used on these goods.   All leather guaranteed for five years.   No roan or sheepskin used because of poor wearing qualities.

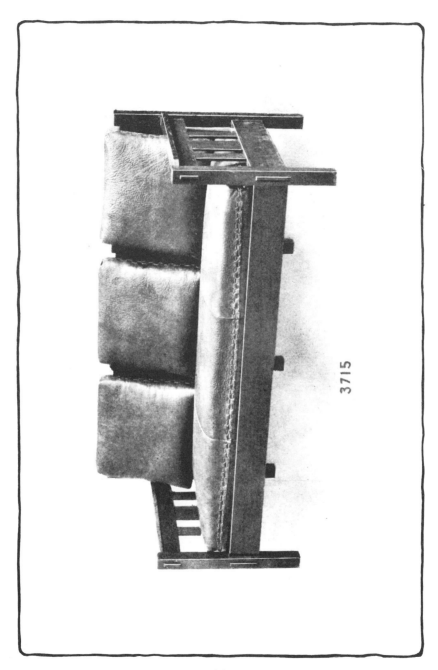

3715

11

NO. 2818 LIBRARY TABLE.

Height, 30 in.; Length, 42 in.; Width, 28 in.
Wood Top.   Oak, $18.00

NO. 2819 LIBRARY TABLE.

Same as above, except top is of Spanish Leather, $28.00

NO. 887 ROCKER.

Height, 34 in.; Width, 20 in.; Depth, 19 in.
Loose Cushion.   Oak, $14.00

NO. 887½ ARM CHAIR.

To match Rocker above, $14.00

NO. 889½ CHAIR.

Height, 36 in.; Width, 19 in.; Depth, 17 in.
Loose Cushion.   Oak, $10.00

NO. 3887 SETTEE.

Height, 38 in.; Length, 48 in.; Depth, 23 in.
Loose Cushion.   Oak, $29.00

All Oak furniture finished in Fumed Oak or any other finish desired.

Spanish Morocco Leather made from Goat and Calfskin is the only leather used on these goods. All leather guaranteed for five years. No roan or sheepskin used because of poor wearing qualities.

887½

887

2818

889½

3887

NO. 3861 SETTEE.

Height, 39 in.; Length, 62 in.; Depth, 25 in.
Loose Seat Cushion and Upholstered Back.   Oak, $39.00

NO. 790 ROCKER.

Height, 36 in.; Width, 19 in.; Depth, 20 in.
Loose Seat Cushion and Upholstered Back.   Oak, $19.00

NO. 790½ ARM CHAIR.

To match Rocker above, $19.00

NO. 792½ CHAIR.

Height, 38 in.; Width, 19 in.; Depth, 17 in.
Loose Seat Cushion and Upholstered Back.   Oak, $13.00

All Oak furniture finished in Fumed Oak or any other finish desired.

Spanish Morocco Leather made from Goat and Calfskin is the only leather used on these goods. All leather guaranteed for five years. No roan or sheepskin used because of poor wearing qualities.

3861

792½

790½

790

NO. 401 COUCH.

Length, 78 in.; Width, 29 in.; Height, 25 in.
Loose Cushions.   Oak, $60.00

All Oak furniture finished in Fumed Oak or any other finish desired.

Spanish Morocco Leather made from Goat and Calfskin is the only leather used on these goods. All leather guar-anteed for five years. No roan or sheepskin used because of poor wearing qualities.

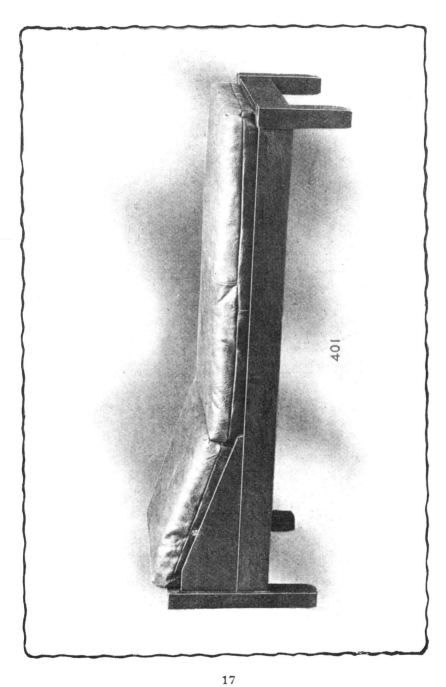

401

NO. 5673 TABOURETTE.

Height, 22 in.; Top, 15 x 15 in.

Wood Top.   Oak, $7.50

NO. 613½ CHAIR.

Height, 35 in.; Seat, 19 x 16 in.

Flag Seat.   Oak, $8.00

No. 613 Rocker to match above,   8.00

NO. 2504 TABLE.

Height, 30 in.; Top, 26 x 26 in.

Wood Top.   Oak, $7.00

NO. 2816 LIBRARY TABLE.

Height, 30 in.; Top, 28 x 42 in.

Copper Trim. Wood Top.   Oak, $20.00

NO. 2817 LIBRARY TABLE.

Same as above except Spanish Leather top, $30.00

NO. 910 ROCKER.

Height, 35 in.; Width, 20 in..; Depth, 20 in.

Loose Seat Cushion.   Oak, $15.00

No. 910½ Arm Chair to match above,   15.00

All Oak furniture finished in Fumed Oak or any other finish desired.

Spanish Morocco Leather made from Goat and Calfskin is the only leather used on these goods. All leather guaranteed for five years. No roan or sheepskin used because of poor wearing qualities.

613½

910

2816

910½

2504

5673

NO. 2812 TABLE.

Height, 30 in.; Top, 22 x 24 in.
Solid Copper Trimmings, Wood Top.   Oak, $11.00

NO. 6566 TABLE DESK.

Height of Writing Bed, 30 in.; Top, 23 x 36 in.
Copper Trimmings, Wood Top.   Oak, $23.00

No. 715½ ARM CHAIR.

Height, 34 in.; Width, 22 in.; Depth, 20 in.
Hand Laced Loose Seat and Back Cushions,   Oak, $42.00
No. 715 Arm Rocker to match above,   42.00

NO. 891 ROCKER.

Height, 40 in.; Width, 19 in.; Depth, 19 in.
Loose Seat Cushion.   Oak, $16.00
No. 891½ Arm Chair to match above,   16.00

NO. 3889 SETTEE.

Height, 37 in.; Depth, 26 in.; Length, 62 in.
Loose Seat Cushion.   Oak, $38.00

All oak furniture finished in Fumed Oak or any other finish desired.

Spanish Morocco Leather made from Goat and Calfskin is the only leather used on these goods. All leather guaranteed for five years. No roan or sheepskin used because of poor wearing qualities.

2812

715½

3889

891

6566

NO. 324½ STOOL.

Height, 9 in.; Top, 13 x 19 in.

Upholstered.

Oak, $5.00

NO. 2615 DEN OR CAFE TABLE.

Height, 28 in.; Top, 18 x 18 in.

Beaten Copper Top.

Oak, $9.00

NO. 277 ROCKER.

Height, 33 in.; Width, 18 in.; Depth, 18 in.

Upholstered Seat.

Oak, $10.00

No. 277½ Arm Chair to match above, 10.00

NO. 615 ROCKER.

Height, 32 in.; Width, 19 in.; Depth, 18 in.

Flag Seat.

Oak, $11.00

No. 615½ Arm Chair to match above, 11.00

NO. 4756 BOOKCASE.

Height, 57 in.; Width, 36 in.; Depth, 12 in.

Copper Trimmings.

Oak, $27.00

NO. 2686 LIBRARY TABLE.

Height, 30 in.; Top, 30 x 46 in.

Copper Trimmings.

Oak, $27.00

All Oak furniture finished in Fumed Oak or any other finish desired.

Spanish Morocco Leather made from Goat and Calfskin is the only leather used on these goods. All leather guaranteed for five years. No roan or sheepskin used because of poor wearing qualities.

2615

324½

615

4756

2686

277

NO. 718½ CHAIR.

Height, 39 in.; Width, 16 in.; Depth, 13 in.
Wood Seat.   Oak, $5.50

NO. 615½ CHAIR.

Height, 35 in.; Width, 19 in.; Depth, 18 in.
Flag Seat.   Oak, $11.00
No. 615 Arm Rocker to match above,   11.00

NO. 2720 HALL TABLE.

Height, 30 in.; Top, 20 x 36 in.
Copper Trimmings, Wood Top.   Oak, $14.00

NO. 2606 TABLE.

Height, 30 in.; Top, 24 x 36 in.
Copper Trimmings, Wood Top.   Oak, $16.00

NO. 6524 OFFICE OR LIBRARY DESK.

Height, 31 in.; Top, 27 x 50 in.
Copper Trimmings.   Oak, $64.00

NO. 6526 OFFICE OR LIBRARY DESK.

Top, 32 x 60 in.
Same construction and finish as above.   Oak, $80.00

All Oak furniture finished in Fumed Oak or any other finish desired.

Spanish Morocco Leather made from Goat and Calfskin is the only leather used on these goods. All leather guaranteed for five years. No roan or sheepskin used because of poor wearing qualities.

2606

718½

615½

2720

6524

NO. 314½ TABOURETTE.

Height, 18 in.; Top, 15 x 15 in.

Wood Top.   Oak, $4.50

NO. 413½ CHAIR.

Height, 38 in.; Width, 19 in.; Depth, 18 in.

Upholstered Seat.   Oak, $12.50

No. 413 Arm Rocker to match above,   12.50

NO. 4602 MAGAZINE RACK.

Height, 51 in.; Width, 16 in.; Depth, 13 in.

Oak, $10.50

NO. 2676 SUTHERLAND TABLE.

Height, 29 in.; Top, 34 x 39 in.

Folding Leaves, Wood Top.   Oak, $15.00

NO. 2680 LIBRARY TABLE.

Height, 30 in.; Top, 36 x 60 in.

Copper Trimmings, Wood Top.   Oak, $56.00

All Oak furniture finished in Fumed Oak or any other finish desired.

Spanish Morocco Leather made from Goat and Calfskin is the only leather used on these goods. All leather guaranteed for five years. No roan or sheepskin used because of poor wearing qualities.

314½

413½

2676

4602

2680

NO. 641 ROCKER.

Height, 37 in.; Width, 23 in.; Depth, 20 in.
Hand Laced Loose Seat and Back Cushions.   Oak, $48.00
No. 641½ Arm Chair to match above,   48.00

NO. 354 MORRIS CHAIR.

Height, 39 in.; Width, 23 in.; Depth, 21 in.
Hand Laced Loose Seat and Back Cushions.   Oak, $49.00

NO. 715 ROCKER.

Height, 34 in.; Width, 22 in.; Depth, 20 in.
Hand Laced Loose Seat and Back Cushions.   Oak, $42.00
No. 715½ Arm Chair to match above,   42.00

NO. 916 ROCKER.

Height, 35 in.; Width, 19 in.; Depth, 18 in.
Loose Seat and Back Cushions.   Oak, $22.00
No. 916½ Arm Chair to match above,   22.00

NO. 917½ CHAIR.

Height, 38 in.; Width, 23 in.; Depth, 21 in.
Loose Seat and Back Cushions.   Oak, $39.00

NO. 289½ CHAIR.

Height, 36 in.; Width, 26 in.; Depth, 21 in.
Hand Laced Loose Seat and Back Cushions.   Oak, $48.00

All Oak furniture finished in Fumed Oak or any other finish desired.

Spanish Morocco Leather made from Goat and Calfskin is the only leather used on these goods. All leather guaranteed for five years. No roan or sheepskin used because of poor wearing qualities.

916

917½

641

354

289½

715

NO. 291½ CHAIR.

Height, 34 in.; Width, 15 in.; Depth, 14 in.
Flag Seat.   Oak, $5.50

NO. 379½ DINING CHAIR.

Height, 37 in.; Width, 18 in.; Depth, 15 in.
Upholstered Seat.   Oak, $6.50

NO. 380½ ARM DINING CHAIR.

Height, 39 in.; Width, 20 in.; Depth, 17 in.
Upholstered Seat.   Oak, $9.50

NO. 933 SEWING ROCKER.

Height, 34 in.; Width, 20 in.; Depth, 16 in.
Loose Seat Cushion.   Oak, $10.00

NO. 873½ CHAIR.

Height, 37 in.; Width, 19 in.; Depth, 19 in.
Loose Seat Cushion.   Oak, $13.00
No. 873 Arm Rocker to match above,   13.00

NO. 3873 SETTEE.

Height, 38 in.; Width, 45 in.; Depth, 23 in.
Loose Seat Cushion.   Oak, $26.00

All Oak furniture finished in Fumed Oak or any other finish desired.

Spanish Morocco Leather made from Goat and Calfskin is the only leather used on these goods. All leather guaranteed for five years. No roan or sheepskin used because of poor wearing qualities.

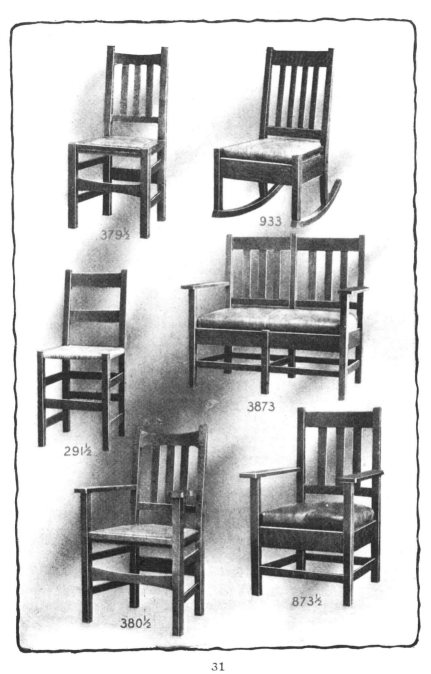

379½

933

291½

3873

380½

873½

NO. 138 TABOURETTE.

Height, 18 in.; Top, 14 x 14 in.
Wood Top. Oak, $4.50

NO. 335 ROTARY CHAIR.

Height, 38 in.; Width, 21 in.; Depth, 19 in.
Saddle Seat. Oak, $16.00
No. 335½ Arm Chair to match above, 10.00

NO. 267 ROCKER.

Height, 36 in.; Width, 19 in.; Depth, 20 in.
Loose Seat Cushion, Full Spring Seat.
Oak, $19.00
Mahogany, 25.00
No. 267½ Arm Chair to match above, Mahogany only, 25.00

NO. 277½ CHAIR.

Height, 37 in.; Width, 18 in.; Depth, 18 in.
Upholstered Seat. Oak, $10.00

NO. 322 ROCKER.

Height, 40 in.; Width, 20 in.; Depth, 20 in.
Hand Laced Loose Seat and Back Cushions. Oak, $37.00
No. 322½ Arm Chair to match above, 37.00

NO. 2534 LIBRARY TABLE.

Height, 30 in.; Top, 30 x 48 in.
Copper Trimmings, Wood Top. Oak, $57.00

NO. 2535 LIBRARY TABLE.

Same size and construction as above, with Spanish
Leather Top, $72.00

All Oak furniture finished in Fumed Oak or any other finish desired.

Spanish Morocco Leather made from Goat and Calfskin is the only leather used on these goods. All leather guaranteed for five years. No roan or sheepskin used because of poor wearing qualities.

277½

138

335

2534

267

322

NO. 727 ROCKER.

Height, 34 in.; Width, 19 in.; Depth, 20 in.
Upholstered Seat.   Oak, $9.50
No. 727½ Arm Chair to match above,   9.50

NO. 175 COSTUMER.

Height, 72 in.; Length of Base, 24 in.; Width, 16 in.
Copper Trimmings.   Oak, $11.50

NO. 171 TABLE DESK.

Height of Writing Bed, 30 in.; Top, 23 x 36 in.
Copper Trimmings, Wood Top.   Oak, $19.00

NO. 2722 LIBRARY TABLE.

Height, 30 in.; Top, 38 x 66 in.
Copper Trimmings, Wood Top.   Oak, $75.00

All Oak furniture finished in Fumed Oak or any other finish desired.

Spanish Morocco Leather made from Goat and Calfskin is the only leather used on these goods. All leather guaranteed for five years. No roan or sheepskin used because of poor wearing qualities.

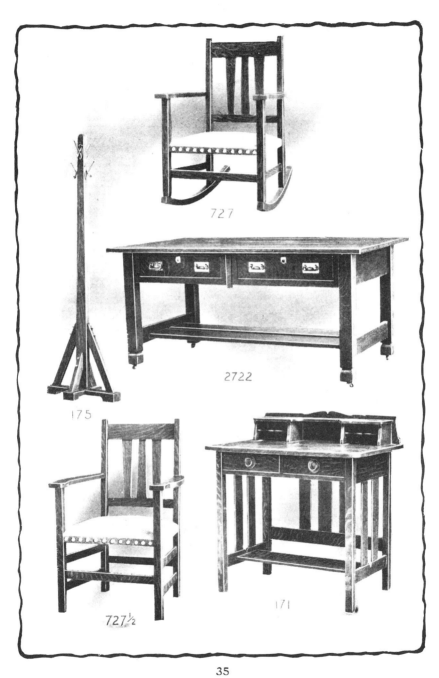

727

2722

175

727½

171

NO. 929½ CHAIR.

Height, 38 in.; Width, 18 in.; Depth, 15 in.
Flag Seat. Oak, $9.00
No. 929 Rocker to match above, 9.00

NO. 2804 LIBRARY TABLE.

Height, 30 in.; Top, 28 x 42 in.
Copper Trimmings, Wood Top. Oak, $29.00

NO. 2805 LIBRARY TABLE.

Same size and construction as above.
Spanish Leather Top. Oak, $42.00

NO. 9017 DRESSER.

Height, 66 in.; Depth, 22 in.; Width, 44 in.
Mirror, 22 x 34 in., Copper Trimmings. Oak, $64.00

NO. 4690 BOOKCASE.

Height, 56 in.; Width, 36 in.; Depth, 13 in.
Copper Trimmings, Two Doors. Oak, $34.00

All Oak furniture finished in Fumed Oak or any other finish desired.

Spanish Morocco Leather made from Goat and Calfskin is the only leather used on these goods. All leather guaranteed for five years. No roan or sheepskin used because of poor wearing qualities.

2804

929½

9017

4690

NO. 833½ FOOT STOOL.

Height, 15 in.; Top, 12 x 17 in.

Upholstered Top.   Oak, $7.00

NO. 602½ DESK CHAIR.

Height, 39 in.; Width, 15 in.; Depth, 14 in.

Saddle Seat.   Oak, $7.50

NO. 187 COSTUMER.

Height, 68 in.; Base, 22 x 22 in.

Copper Trimmings.   Oak, $8.00

NO. 188 COSTUMER.

Height, 68 in.; Base, 18 x 20 in.

Copper Trimmings.   Oak, $12.00

NO. 2530 LIBRARY TABLE.

Height, 30 in.; Top, 28 x 48 in.

Copper Trimmings, Wood Top.   Oak, $42.00

All Oak furniture finished in Fumed Oak or any other finish desired.

Spanish Morocco Leather made from Goat and Calfskin is the only leather used on these goods. All leather guaranteed for five years. No roan or sheepskin used because of poor wearing qualities.

187

833½

188

602½

2530

NO. 394½ FOOT STOOL.

Height, 17 in.; Top, 14 x 20 in.
Hand Laced Loose Cushion.   Oak, $11.00

NO. 130 TABLE.

Height, 30 in.; Top, 40 x 40 in.
Wood Top.   Oak, $20.00

NO. 181 TABLE.

Same construction and size as above.
Spanish Leather Top.   Oak, $32.00

NO. 412½ DINING CHAIR.

Height, 37 in.; Width, 19½ in.; Depth, 16 in.
Upholstered Seat.   Oak, $9.50

NO. 413½ ARM DINING CHAIR.

To match above.   Oak, $12.50

NO. 281 ROCKER.

Height, 38 in.; Width, 20 in.; Depth, 20 in.
Upholstered Seat.   Oak, $13.00
No. 281½ Arm Chair to match above,   13.00

NO. 285½ ARM CHAIR.

Height, 41 in.; Width, 20 in.; Depth, 20 in.
Upholstered Seat.   Oak, $12.00
No. 285 Arm Rocker to match above,   12.00

NO. 6500 WRITING DESK.

Height, 48 in.; Width, 36 in.; Depth, 14 in.
Height of Writing Bed, 30 in.   Copper Trimmings.
Natural Walnut Pigeon Hole Work.   Oak, $34.00

All Oak furniture finished in Fumed Oak or any other finish desired.

Spanish Morocco Leather made from Goat and Calfskin is the only leather used on these goods. All leather guaranteed for five years. No roan or sheepskin used because of poor wearing qualities.

130

285½

412½

6500

281

394½

NO. 283½ DESK CHAIR.

Height, 39 in.; Width, 16 in.; Depth, 13 in.
Saddle Seat.   Oak, $6.50

NO. 604½ DESK CHAIR.

Height, 39 in.; Width, 17 in.; Depth, 14 in.
Saddle Seat.   Oak, $8.50

NO. 2724 TABLE.

Height, 30 in.; Top, 28 x 28 in.
Folding Leaves, Wood Top.   Oak, $10.00

NO. 137 TABLE.

Height, 30 in.; Top, 24 x 24 in.
Wood Top.   Oak, $7.50

NO. 7578 HANGING GLASS.

Mirror, 12 x 20 in.
Copper Trimming.   Oak, $12.00

NO. 3578 SETTEE.

Height, 36 in.; Length, 40 in.; Depth, 19 in.
Copper Trimming, Wood Seat.   Oak, $15.00

All Oak furniture finished in Fumed Oak or any other
finish desired.

Spanish Morocco Leather made from Goat and Calfskin
is the only leather used on these goods. All leather guaranteed for five years. No roan or sheepskin used because
of poor wearing qualities.

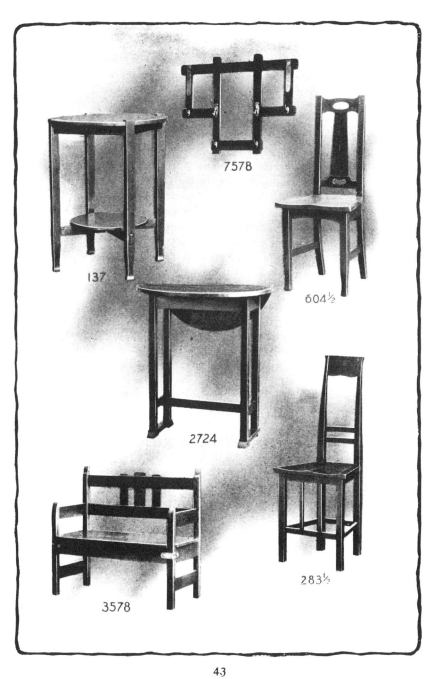

7578

137

604½

2724

3578

283½

NO. 3263 SETTEE.

Height, 35 in.; Length, 63 in.; Depth, 28 in.
Loose Seat and Back Cushions. Full Spring Seat.

Solid Mahogany, $90.00
Natural Walnut,   90.00

The Walnut goods are made from selected, solid
American Black Walnut (no veneers) and finished in a
light gray tone—perfectly natural. Dull finish.

Russian Morocco Leather made from Goatskin is the
only leather used on these goods. All leather guaranteed
for five years. No roan or sheepskin used because of poor
wearing qualities.

3263

NO. 263 ROCKER.

Height, 35 in.; Width, 24 in.; Depth, 20 in.
Loose Seat and Back Cushion, Full Spring Seat.

Solid Mahogany,	$50.00
Natural Walnut,	50.00

No. 263½ Arm Chair to match above.
Price, construction and finish same as above.

NO. 265½ CHAIR.

Height, 38 in.; Width, 17 in.; Depth, 15 in.
Upholstered Seat.

Solid Mahogany,	$14.00
Natural Walnut,	14.00

NO. 2806 LIBRARY TABLE.

Height, 30 in.; Top, 33 x 48 in.
Dull Brass Trimmings.

Solid Mahogany,		$52.00
Natural Walnut,		52.00
Copper Trimmings.	Oak,	34.00

NO. 6800 TABLE DESK.

Height of Writing Bed, 30 in.; Top, 24 x 36 in.
Dull Brass Trimmings.

Solid Mahogany,		$37.00
Natural Walnut,		37.00
Copper Trimmings.	Oak,	27.00

The Walnut goods are made from selected, solid American Black Walnut (no veneers) and finished in a light gray tone—perfectly natural. Dull finish.

Russia Morocco Leather made from Goatskin is the only leather used on these goods. All leather guaranteed for five years. No roan or sheepskin used because of poor wearing qualities.

6800

263½

2806

263

265½

NO. 4804 MAGAZINE STAND.

Height, 36 in.; Top, 15 x 20 in.

Oak,	$11.00
Solid Mahogany,	16.00
Natural Walnut,	16.00

NO. 9022 CHIFFONIER.

Height, 53 in.; Width, 36 in.; Depth, 18 in.
Copper Trimmings.   Oak, $72.00

NO. 9000 BEDSTEAD.

Height of Head. 51 in.; Slats, 3 ft. 6 in.
Height of Foot, 45 in.; Rails, 6 ft. 4 in.

Oak, $30.00

NO. 9000½ BEDSTEAD.

Finish and construction same as above, except,
Slats, 4 ft. 6 in.   Oak, $34.00

NO. 9004 BEDSTEAD.

Height of Head, 50 in.; Slats, 3 ft. 6 in.
Height of Foot, 42 in.; Rails, 6 ft. 4 in.

Oak, $34.00

NO. 9004½ BEDSTEAD.

Finish and construction same as above, except,
Slats, 4 ft. 6 in.   Oak, $38.00

All Oak furniture finished in Fumed Oak or any other finish desired.

Spanish Morocco Leather made from Goat and Calfskin is the only leather used on these goods. All leather guaranteed for five years. No roan or sheepskin used because of poor wearing qualities.

4804

9000

9004

9022

NO. 347½ ARM CHAIR.

Height, 46 in.; Width, 20 in.; Depth, 20 in.
Upholstered Seat and Back.   Oak, $23.00
No. 347 Arm Rocker to match above,   23.00

NO. 301 ARM ROCKER.

Height, 37 in.; Width, 19 in.; Depth, 19 in.
Loose Cushion and Upholstered Back.   Oak, $25.00
No. 301½ Arm Chair to match above,   25.00

NO. 3301 SETTEE.

Height, 38 in.; Length, 62 in.; Depth, 28 in.
Loose Cushion and Upholstered Back.   Oak, $56.00

All Oak furniture finished in Fumed Oak or any other finish desired.

Spanish Morocco Leather made from Goat and Calfskin is the only leather used on these goods. All leather guaranteed for five years. No roan or sheepskin used because of poor wearing qualities.

301

347½

3301

NO. 8637 SERVING TABLE.

Height, 32 in.; Top, 20 x 42 in.

Copper Trimmings, Wood Top.   Oak, $20.00

NO. 2640 EXTENSION TABLE.

Height, 30 in.; Top, 54 x 54 in.

Oak, Extension, 8 ft., $38.00
Oak, Extension, 10 ft.,   44.00

NO. 8745 CHINA CLOSET.

Height, 61 in.; Width, 32 in.; Depth, 14 in.

Copper Trimmings, Two Doors.   Oak, $34.00

NO. 8743 CHINA CLOSET.

Same as above, except width, 30 in., and Single Door, $30.00

NO. 8707 SIDEBOARD.

Height, 45 in.; Length, 48 in.; Depth, 22 in.

Copper Trimmings.   Oak, $52.00

All Oak furniture finished in Fumed Oak or any other finish desired.

Spanish Morocco Leather made from Goat and Calfskin is the only leather used on these goods. All leather guaranteed for five years. No roan or sheepskin used because of poor wearing qualities.

8637

8707

8745

2640

NO. 7568 PLATE RACK.

Height, 21 in.; Length, 48 in.

Oak, $13.00

NO. 8610 BUFFET.

Height, 47 in.; Length, 54 in.; Depth, 21 in.
Copper Trimmings.   Oak, $56.00

NO. 8644 CHINA CLOSET.

Height, 68 in.; Width, 48 in.; Depth, 18 in.
Copper Trimmings.   Oak, $100.00

NO. 8604 SIDEBOARD.

Height, 64 in.; Length, 70 in.; Depth, 22 in.
Copper Trimmings.   Oak, $140.00

All Oak furniture finished in Fumed Oak or any other finish desired.

Spanish Morocco Leather made from Goat and Calfskin is the only leather used on these goods. All leather guaranteed for five years. No roan or sheepskin used because of poor wearing qualities.

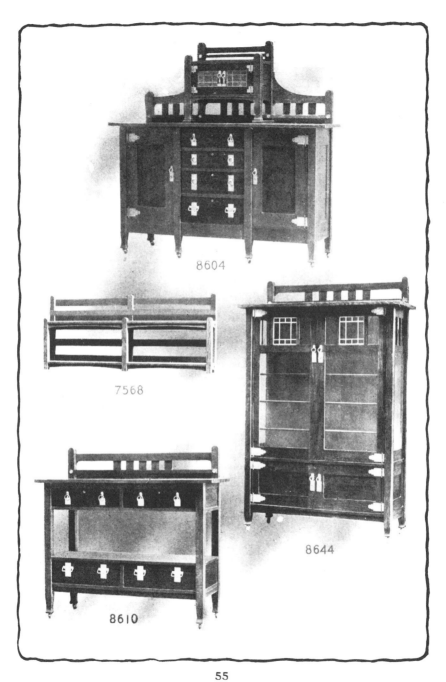

8604

7568

8644

8610

NO. 3899 SETTEE.

Height, 38 in.; Length, 72 in.; Depth, 29 in.
Loose Seat and Back Cushions.   Oak, $70.00

All Oak furniture finished in Fumed Oak or any other finish desired.

Spanish Morocco Leather made from Goat and Calfskin is the only leather used on these goods. All leather guaranteed for five years. No roan or sheepskin used because of poor wearing qualities.

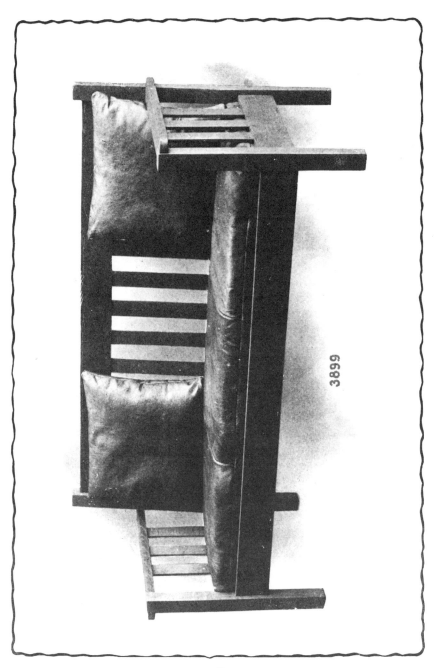

3899

NO. 184 TABLE.

Height, 30 in.; Top, 24 x 36 in.

Wood Top. Oak, $14.50

NO. 541 ROCKER.

Height, 37 in.; Width, 19 in.; Depth, 20 in.
Hand Laced Loose Seat Cushion. Oak, $18.00
No. 541½ Arm Chair to match above, 18.00

NO. 389 ROCKER.

Height, 38 in.; Width, 19 in.; Depth, 21 in.
Loose Seat and Back Cushions. Oak, $28.00
No. 389½ Arm Chair to match above, 28.00

No. 4692 BOOKCASE.

Height, 56 in.; Width, 48 in.; Depth, 12 in.
Copper Trimmings, Two Doors.

Oak, $46.00
Mahogany, 60.00
Walnut, 60.00

All Oak furniture finished in Fumed Oak or any other finish desired.

Spanish Morocco Leather made from Goat and Calfskin is the only leather used on these goods. All leather guaranteed for five years. No roan or sheepskin used because of poor wearing qualities.

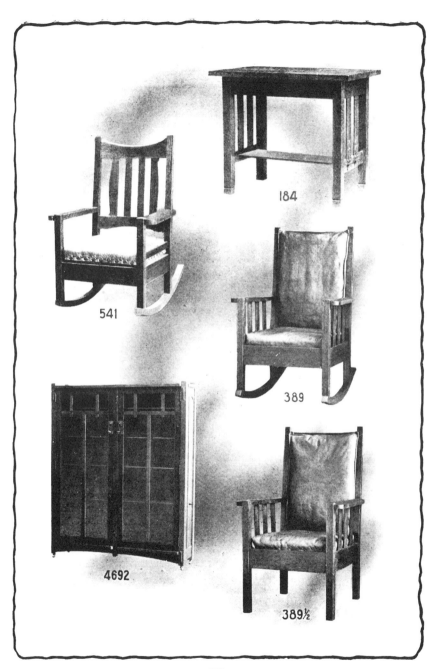

184

541

389

4692

389½

59

NO. 651½ DINING CHAIR.

Height, 25 in.; Width, 17 in.; Depth, 15 in.

Upholstered Seat.   Oak, $8.50

Also made in Flag Seat (No. 885½),   8.50

NO. 651¼ ARM CHAIR.

Made to match No. 651½ Dining Chair, $11.50

Also made in Flag Seat (No. 885¼),   11.50

NO. 8733 SERVING TABLE.

Height, 30 in.; Top, 22 x 34 in.

Oak, $9.00

NO. 8703 SIDEBOARD.

Height, 46 in.; Length, 48 in.; Depth, 22 in.

Copper Trimmings.   Oak, $44.00

NO. 8605 SIDEBOARD.

Height, 55 in.; Length, 60 in.; Depth, 23 in.

Copper Trimmings.   Oak, $70.00

All Oak furniture finished in Fumed Oak or any other finish desired.

Spanish Morocco Leather made from Goat and Calfskin is the only leather used on these goods. All leather guaranteed for five years. No roan or sheepskin used because of poor wearing qualities.

8703

651¼

8733

651½

8605

NO. 311 ELECTROLIER.

Height over all, 24 in.; Diameter of Top, 24 in.
Diameter of Base, 18 in.
Bent Stained Art Glass. 8—16 C. P. Opalescent Lights.
Bead Fringe. All Copper. $150.00

311

NO. 135 CANDLESTICK.

Height, 10 in.; Diameter of Base, 5 in. $4.00

NO. 325 CANDELABRA.

Height, 13 in.; Diameter of Base, 6 in.
Brass Trimmings. 16 C. P. Light.
Shade, Red or Yellow. $11.00

NO. 344 ELECTRIC SCONCE.

Height, 15 in.; Width, 9 in.; Extension from Wall, 3 in.
2—16 C. P. Lights. $15.00

NO. 314 TABLE LAMP.

Height, 18 in.; Diameter of Top, 11 in.
Brass and Iron Trimmings. 6 in. 16 C. P. Light. $40.00

NO. 163 ELECTRIC CANDELABRA.

Height, 18 in.; Width, 16 in.; Base, 7½ x 9½ in.
2—16 C. P. Lights. $26.00

NO. 145 CANDELABRA.

Height, 13 in.; Width, 12 in.; Base, 6 x 6 in.
Brass Trimmings. $14.50

NO. 310 ELECTROLIER.

Height, 30 in.; Top, 24 x 24 in.; Base, 18 x 18 in.
Stained Art Glass, 8—16 C. P. Lights. $80.00

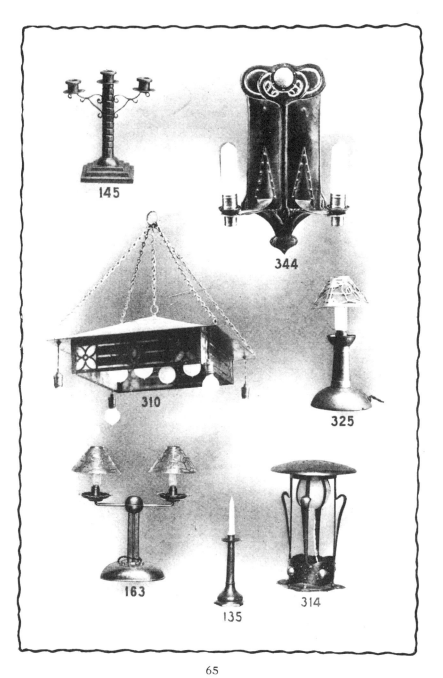

145

344

310

325

163

135

314

NO. 147 CANDLESTICK.

Height, 6 in.; Base, 5 x 5 in.; Brass Rivets. $5.00

NO. 137 CANDLESTICK.

Height, 8 in.; Diameter Base, 6 in. $5.00

NO. 131 CANDLESTICK.

Height, 13½ in.; Diameter Base, 4 in.
Brass Rings and Top. $4.50

NO. 128 TEAPOT.

Height, 9 in.; Diameter, 4½ in.
Tinned inside for practical use. $7.00

NO. 144 TOBACCO JAR.

Height, 7½ in.; Diameter, 5½ in.
Base and Center are Brass, Zinc Lined. $9.50

NO. 168 UMBRELLA RACK.

Height, 27 in.; Extreme Diameter, 12½ in.
Diameter of Opening, 8 in. Base, Brass. $24.00

NO. 36 PLAQUE.

Diameter, 14 in. $9.00

NO. 300 ELECTROLIER.

Extreme Height, 42 in.; Diameter, 30 in.
Diameter Brass Ball, 10 in.; Diameter Bells, 8 in.
5—16 C. P. Lights. $120.00

NO. 174 ELECTRIC CANDELABRA.

Height, 12 in.; Diameter Base, 5 in.
8 C. P. Lights, Miniature. $10.00

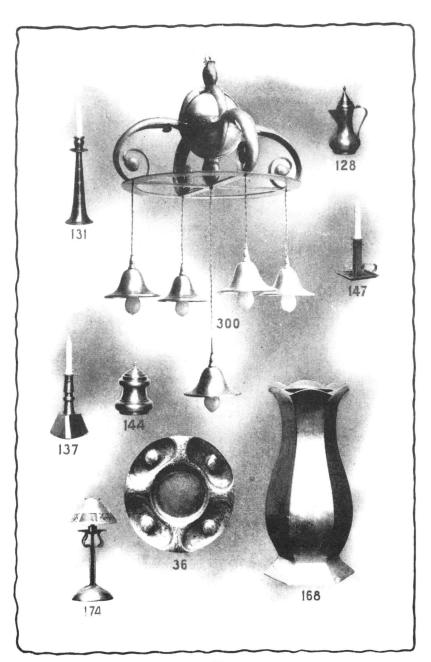

131

128

147

300

137

144

174

36

168

NO. 84 CANDLESTICK.

Height, 10 in.; Width, 5½ in.

Brass Trimmings. $5.00

NO. 304 ELECTROLIER.

Extreme Height, 30 in.; Extreme Diameter, 21 in.
Diameter Brass Ball, 10 in.; Diameter Bells, 10 in.
2½ in. Opalescent 16 C. P. Lights. $100.00

NO. 178 CANDLESTICK.

Height, 10 in.; Diameter of Base, 5½ in. $7.50

NO. 175 CANDELABRA.

Height, 13 in.; Diameter of Base, 5 in.
Copper or Brass. 16 C. P. Light. $10.50

NO. 358 SIDE LIGHT.

Height, 12 in.; Spread, 13 in.; Extension from Wall, 7½ in.
Diameter of Shade, 3 in. 16 C. P. Lights. $27.00

NO. 318 TABLE LAMP.

Height, 19 in.; Spread of Top, 15 in.
Bead Fringe. 3—16 C. P. Lights.

Brass and Copper. $50.00

NO. 316 TABLE LAMP.

Height, 18 in.; Spread of Top, 15 in.
Bead Fringe. 3—16 C. P. Lights.

All Copper. $60.00

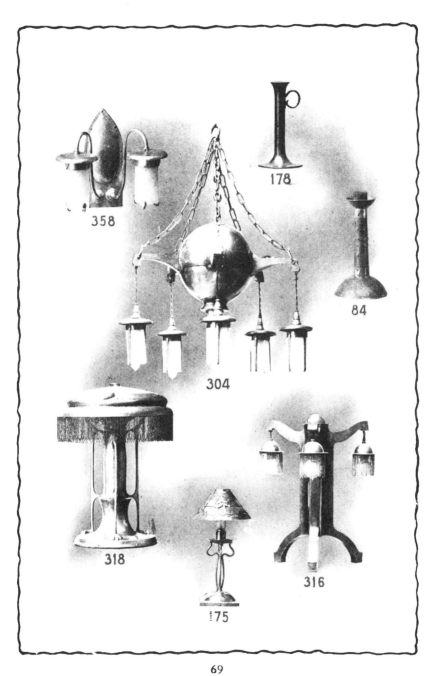

358

178

84

304

318

175

316

NO. 71 JARDINIERE.

Height, 6½ in.; Width of Opening, 10 in. $16.00

NO. 72 PLAQUE.

Diameter, 16 in. $9.00

NO. 18 JARDINIERE.

Height, 12½ in.; Base, 10 x 10 in.
Extreme Width, 14 in.; Width of Opening, 11 in.
Depth of Pan, 10 in.   Removable Pan.
Brass Trimmings and Corners. $32.00

NO. 119 SEVENTEENTH CENTURY FIREPOT.

Height, 18½ in.; Diameter, 11 in.
Brass Trimmings and Top. $20.00

NO. 166 JARDINIERE.

Height, 16 in.; Diameter, 20½ in.
Diameter of Opening, 16 in.
Brass Rim. $60.00

71

72

166

119

18

NO. 40 FINGER BOWL.

Width, 5 in.; Depth, 2 in. $1.50

NO. 116 COAL BUCKET.

Height, 16 in.; Diameter, 13½ in.
Iron Handles, Brass Base. $16.00

NO. 96 UMBRELLA STAND.

Height, 28 in.; Diameter, 12 in.; Diameter Opening, 7½ in.
Brass Trimmings. $30.00

NO. 97 UMBRELLA STAND.

Height, 29 in.; Diameter, 14½ in.
Diameter Opening, 10 in. $40.00

NO. 167 UMBRELLA STAND.

Height, 26 in.; Diameter, 10 in.
Base, Brass. $15.00

NO. 180 UMBRELLA STAND.

Height, 26 in.; Diameter, 10 in.; Diameter Opening, 6 in.
Base, Brass. $17.00

NO. 77 SERVING TRAY.

Length, 23 in.; Width, 12 in. $15.00

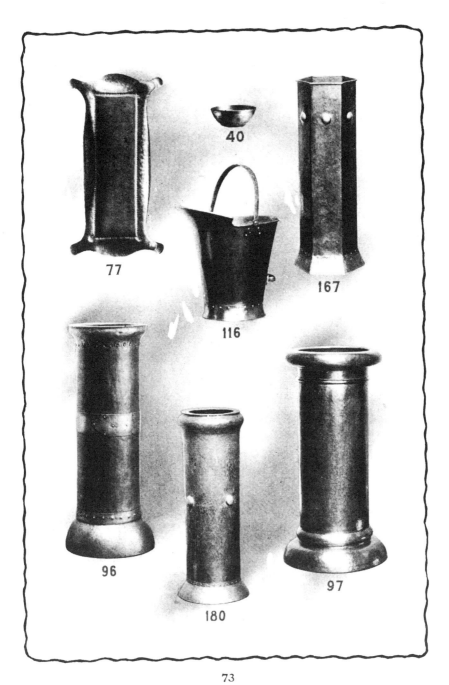

77

40

167

116

96

180

97

73

NO. 199 PAPER CUTTER.
Length, 13 in.
Brass Handle, Copper Blade. $4.00

NO. 200 PAPER CUTTER.
Length, 13½ in.
Brass Handle, Copper Blade. $8.00

NO. 31 PITCHER.
Height, 12 in.; Width of Bowl, 6 in.
Brass Trimming. $10.00

NO. 73 PITCHER.
Height, 15 in.; Diameter Base, 5½ in.
Wrought Iron Base. $10.00

NO. 93 LOVING CUP.
Height, 9 in.; Diameter, 7 in.
Wrought Iron Handles. $11.00

NO. 122 ALGERIAN WATER PITCHER.
Height, 13 in.; Diameter, 6½ in.
Brass Handle, Tinned Inside. $10.00

NO. 59 TEAPOT.
Height, 10¾ in.; Diameter of Bowl, 7½ in.
Brass Handle, Nickeled Inside. $18.00

NO. 80 WINE PITCHER.
Height, 14 in.; Diameter Base, 6 in.
Wrought Iron Handles. $10.00

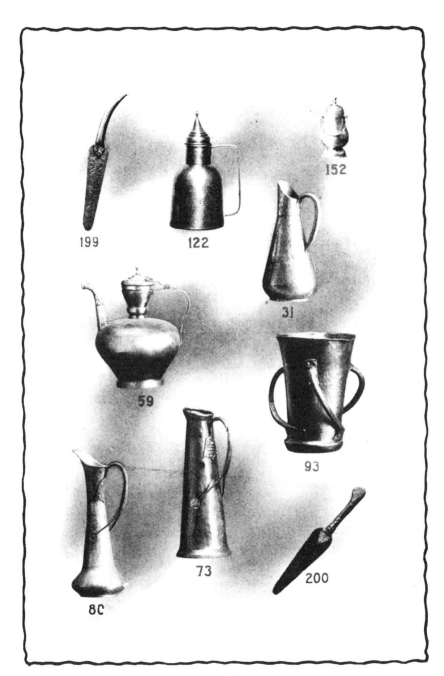

199

122

152

31

59

93

80

73

200

NO. 15 ASH TRAY.

Diameter, 6 in. $1.00

NO. 159 JARDINIERE.

Height, 7 in.; Diameter, 10½ in.; Diameter Opening, 6 in.
Top Rim Brass. $9.00

NO. 25 MUG.

Height, 5¾ in.; Diameter, 4½ in. $3.00

NO. 94 VASE.

Height, 12 in.; Diameter, 9½ in. $17.00

NO. 21 TEAPOT.

Height, 12 in.; Diameter, 12 in.
Brass Handle; Nickeled Inside. $19.00

NO. 90 PITCHER.

Height, 16 in.; Diameter, 6 in.
Brass Handle. $10.00

NO. 185 SMOKING SET.

Tray, 7 x 11 in.; Wood Base.
Cigar Holder, Diameter, 3 in.; Height, 4½ in.
Match Box, Diameter, 2 in.; Height, 2 in.
Alcohol Lamp, Diameter, 2½ in.; Height, 1½ in. $20.00

NO. 150 WOOD BOX.

Height, 18 in.; Inside, 16 x 18 in.
Copper Trimming.   Wrought Iron Handles.

$7.00

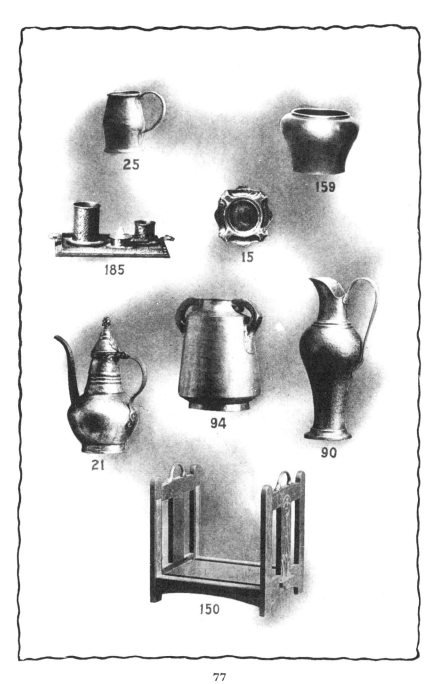

25

159

185

15

21

94

90

150

NO. 16½ ASH TRAY.

Diameter, 6 in. $1.00

No. 179 TOBACCO JAR AND ASH TRAY.

Height of Jar, 8 in.
Diameter of Jar, 4½ in.; Diameter of Tray, 9 in.
Zinc Lined. $11.00

NO. 160 SMOKING SET.

Lamp and Match Safe, 2½ in. high; Cigarette Box, 3 x 4 in.
Cigar Box, 4½ x 4½ in.
Tobacco Jar, 6 x 6½ in. Diameter of Tray, 15 in.
Zinc Lined. $20.00

NO. 64 CIGAR BOX.

Height, 6 in.; Length, 11½ in.; Width, 6¾ in.
Cedar Lined, Brass Trimmings. $20.00

NO. 63 CIGARETTE BOX.

Height, 5¼ in.; Length, 6¾ in.; Width, 5 in.
Cedar Lined, Brass Handle and Legs. $10.00

NO. 172 INK STAND.

Length, 11 in.; Width, 6½ in.; Height of Back, 4 in.
Copper or Brass. $8.00

NO. 173 INK STAND.

Length, 12 in.; Width, 7 in.; Height of Back, 5 in.
Oak Base. $14.00

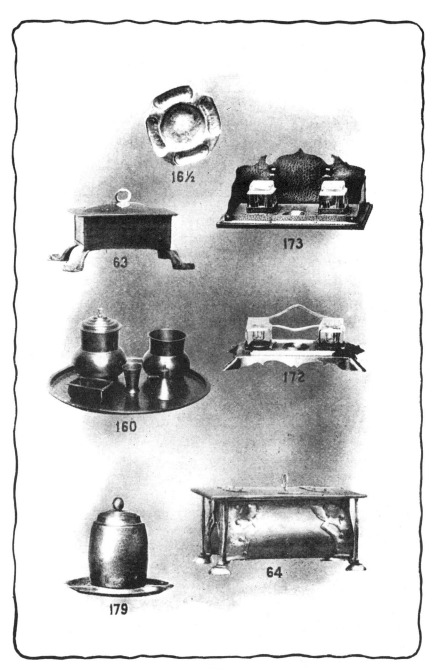

16½

173

63

160

172

64

179